Name:

....

School:

....

Class:

....

ph ph ph ph ph ph

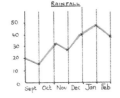

elephant dolphin graphic

microphone phantom photograph

alphabet telephone

Read the words underneath each elephant and draw a picture inside the elephant.

elephant

dolphin

phone

phantom

2

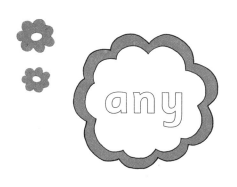

Tricky words

any

many

Write over the dotted letters and add the missing letters.

any   a_y   _ny   an_   _n_

many   m_ny   _a_y   man_

Finish these sentences by adding either *any*, or *many*.

 Have you got _____ milk?

How _____ ducks are in the pond?

Dictation:

_____

_____

Read the tricky words and color the flowers using either red, or green.

what   when   which   why   where   who

Short or long vowel?

Read the words. Decide which word matches each picture and write this word on the line.

ran rain	cot coat	bat bait
fin fine	cub cube	rod road
net neat	kit kite	bed bead

Add the following seaside things to the picture.

Add these seaside things:

1. six fish

2. a big crab

3. a flying seagull

4. a starfish

5. a shark with big teeth

6. three red shells

7. a boat

8. a man in the boat

9. a yellow sun in the sky

excellent   ice   fence   face   circle

pencil   circus   cylinder   cycle   cygnet

Read the words and write them under the matching circus tent. Color the pictures.

ice-cream

ice-cream
fence
circus tent
circle
cygnets
cycle
pencil
face

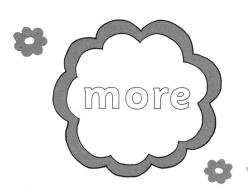  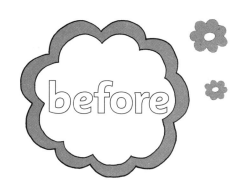

more

Tricky words

before

Write over the dotted letters and add the missing letters.

more   m_re   _or_   mo_e

before   be_or_   __fore   bef__e

Finish these sentences by adding either *more*, or *before*.

I went swimming _____ lunch.

"We need _____ butter," said Dad.

Dictation:

_____

_____

Read the tricky words and color the flowers using a green pen, or pencil.

which   why   where   who   any   many

7

This is me.

Is it true? Write *yes*, or *no* underneath each statement.

The cat is sleeping.

yes

Rabbits are good at hopping.

_____

There are five red socks.

_____

It is three o'clock.

_____

The dragon has ten eggs.

_____

The magpie has a hat.

_____

When the letter ‹g› is followed by ‹e›, ‹i›, or ‹y›, it usually makes a /j/ sound.

Read the words, then write them in the vegetable with the same spelling pattern.

oranges   large   vegetable   germ

giraffe   giant   ginger   magic

gypsy   gym   gymnast   dingy

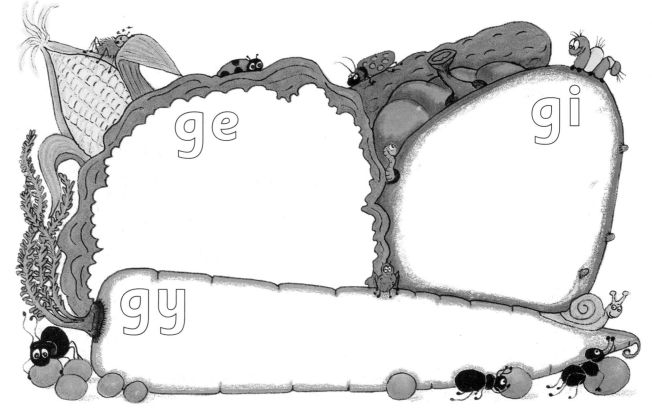

Read the words and illustrate them in the frames.

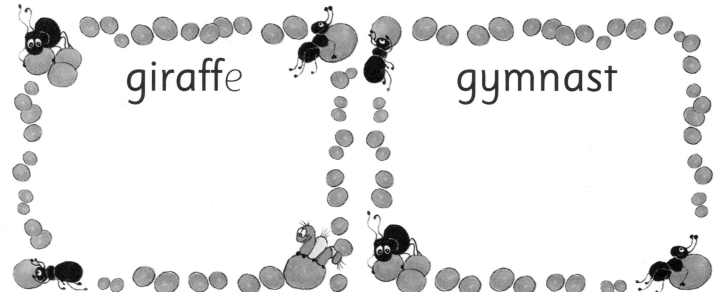

giraffe   gymnast

other   Tricky words   were

Write over the dotted letters and add the missing letters.

other   o__er   _ther   _th__

were   wer_   _e_e   w__e

Finish these sentences by adding either *other*, or *were*.

We _____ skipping in the park.

Jim has lost the _____ sock.

Dictation:

_____

_____

Read the tricky words and color the flowers using a green pen, or pencil.

where   who   any   many   more   before

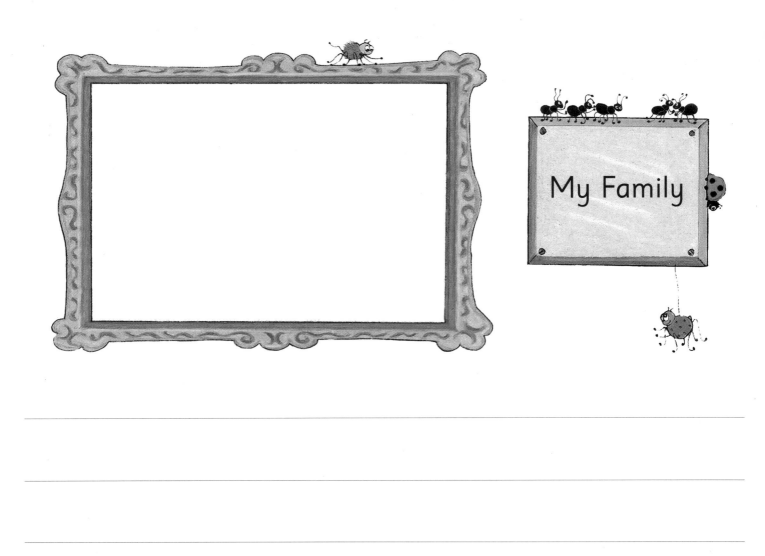

My Family

Read the words and then write them in the correct /ai/ spelling.

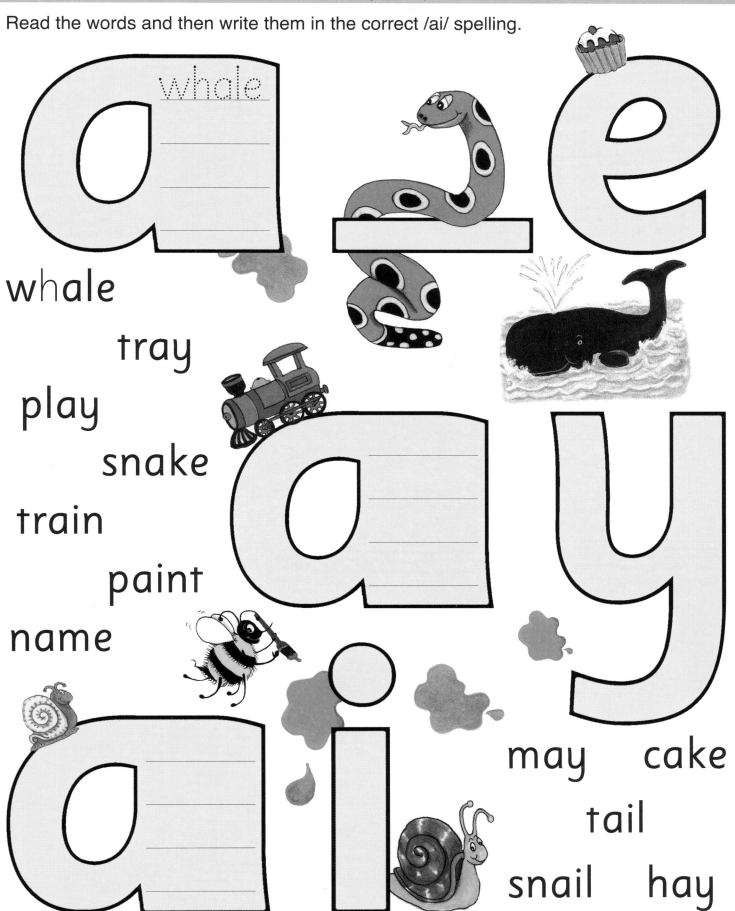

whale

tray

play

snake

train

paint

name

may   cake

tail

snail   hay

13

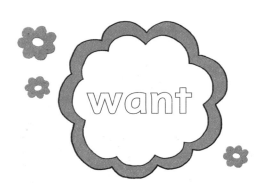

Tricky words

want

because

Write over the dotted letters and add the missing letters.

want   w_nt   _a_t   w_n_

because   b_c_s_   _e_u_e

Finish these sentences by adding either *want*, or *because*.

Do you _____ to help?

He went home _____ he felt sick.

Dictation:

_____

_____

Write inside the outline letters.

big elephants catch ants under small elephants.

14

My House

speed   sneeze 🐝 toffee   indeed

teacher   peanut   peach   seatbelt

eve 🥜 theme   these   Pete

Read the words and then write them in the correct /ee/ spelling.

feet   athlete

beak   eve

theme

sleep

these

feet
_____
_____
_____

_____
_____
_____

teeth
read
seal
bee
tea

_____
_____
_____

16

Tricky words

Write over the dotted letters and add the missing letters.

put   p_t   _u_   p__   ___

saw   s__   _a_   __w   ___

Finish these sentences by adding either *put*, or *saw*.

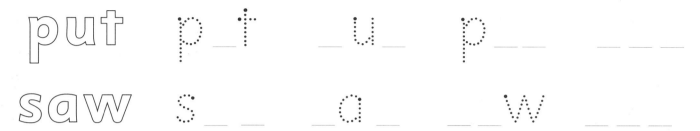

I _____ my drum back in the toy box.

Yesterday, we _____ Dad do a handstand.

Dictation:

_____

_____

Read the tricky words and color the flowers using a green pen, or pencil.

more   before   other   were   want   because

My Best Dinner

_____

_____

_____

_____

_____

_____

_____

Read each phrase and draw a picture in the frame to illustrate it.

a rabbit in a hutch

a big rainbow in the sky

a black cat in red boots

a bat in a tree

the moon and some stars

three snails in the rain

Read the words and write them in the correct /ie/ spelling.

light

fly

like

prize

night

kite

die

light

my

time

right

thigh

reply

lie

sky

pie

tie

could

Tricky words

should

would

Write over the dotted letters and add the missing letters.

could
c _ _ l d
c _ u _ d

should
s h o _ _ d
s h _ _ _ d

would
w o _ l _
w _ u _ d

Finish these sentences by adding *could*, *should*, or *would*.

_____ you like some more tea?

I _____ put the tent up now, if you like.

We _____ clean out the hamster's cage.

Dictation:

_____

_____

_____

Read the tricky words and color the flowers using either green, or pink.

other

were

because

want

saw

put

The animal
I like best
is...

toast   coach   coast   raincoat

tadpole   those   home   joke

rainbow   elbow   snow   window

Read the words and then write them in the correct /oa/ spelling.

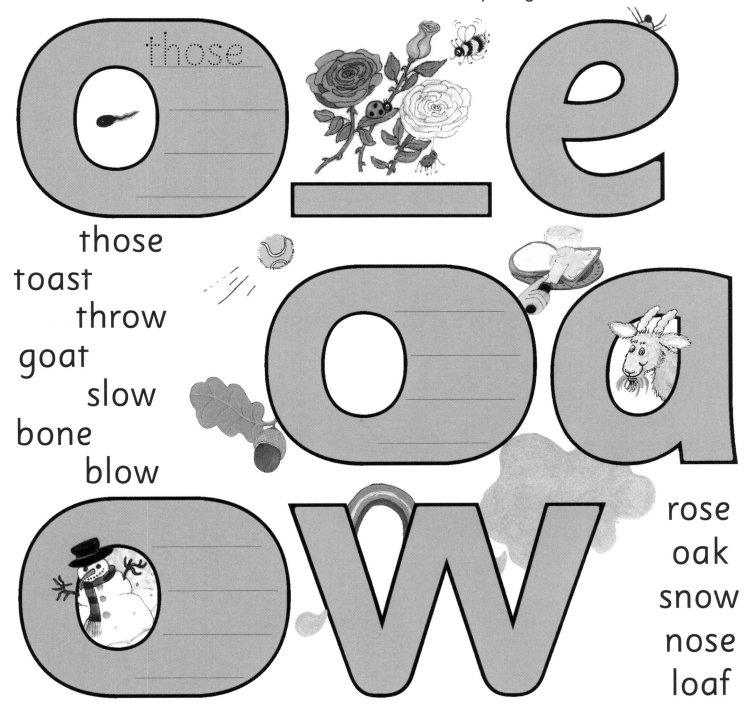

those
toast
throw
goat
slow
bone
blow

those

rose
oak
snow
nose
loaf

23

Write over the dotted letters and add the missing letters.

right   two   four   goes

r _ _ t   t _ _   f _ _ _   g _ _ _

Finish these sentences by adding *right*, *two*, *four*, or *goes*.

He got all the sums _____.

She _____ swimming after school.

 Two plus two is _____.

The _____ boys are twins.

Dictation:

_____

_____

_____

My Best
Day

Read the sentences and fill in the gaps. Color the pictures to match each sentence.

The tall oak ____ is green.

My ____ is long and has red and green stripes.

My blue ____ has a big collar.

The little green ____ jumped into the pond.

The ____ shines in the night.

I found a ____ in the garden.
It had a yellow shell on its back.

26

bluebell   rescue   true   statue

ruler   use   excuse   tune

news   chew   threw   stew

Read the words and then write them in the correct /ue/ spelling.

u_e

cube

ue

ew

cube   cue

argue   few

cute

pew

blew

tune

statue

skew

rescue

mute

does   **Tricky words**   made   their

Write over the dotted letters and add the missing letters.

does   made   their
d _ _ s   m _ d _   th _ _ _
do _ _   m _ _ _   t _ _ _ r

Finish these sentences by adding *does*, *made*, or *their*.

We _____ some cakes yesterday.

They played with _____ dog.

When _____ the match start?

Dictation:

_____

_____

_____

Read the tricky words and color the flowers using a pink pen, or pencil.

should   would   right   two   four   goes

My Game

At the zoo: answer the questions by looking at the zoo picture underneath.

1. How many animals are in the tree? _____

2. Which animal has a trunk? _____

3. What sort of animal is an ostrich? _____

4. Where is the crocodile swimming? _____

5. Who has black and white stripes? _____

6. How many giraffes are there? _____

Make as many words as you can from the letters in the word:

elephants

sheep

_____

_____

_____

_____

_____

flour   about   flower   shower

count   mouse   brown   downhill

found   sound   vowel   clown

Read the words and then write them in the correct /ou/ spelling.

mouse

brown

owl

mouth

cow

found

cloud

clown

ou

mouse

ow

once **upon** Tricky words **always**

Write over the dotted letters and add the missing letters.

once   upon   always

_ n _ _   _ _ on   _ _ way _

_ _ _ e   _ p _ _   _ l _ _ s

Fill in the gaps by adding *once*, *upon*, or *always* and then finish the story.

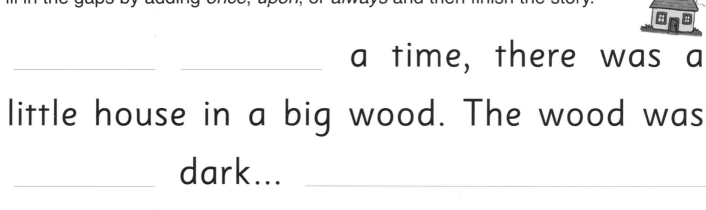

_____ _____ a time, there was a little house in a big wood. The wood was _____ dark... _____

_____

_____

Read the tricky words and color the flowers using a pink pen, or pencil.

four   right   goes   does   made   their

Re-telling a Story

At the park: choose the right word to finish the sentences.

1. The dog is carrying a _____. **stick / stuck**

2. There is a cat in the _____. **shed / tree**

3. The fox is looking at the _____. **robin / rabbit**

4. The ducks _____ on the pond. **quack / quit**

5. The boys have a bat and _____. **ball / wall**

6. The bird is _____. **singing / swinging**

royal   boy   spoil   coin

annoy   enjoy   oil   point

toys   joy   join   boil

Read the words and then write them in the correct /oi/ spelling.

point
_____
_____
_____

point   toy   joy

oil   coin   boy

spoil

enjoy

35

also · of · Tricky words · eight

Write over the dotted letters and add the missing letters.

also   of   eight

__ __ s __   o __   __ __ __ __ t

__ __ __ o   __ __   __ i __ h __

Dictation:

_____

_____

_____

Finish these sentences by adding *also*, *of*, or *eight*.

There are lots _____ sheep on the farm.

I counted _____ chickens in the yard.

There are _____ cows on the farm.

Read the tricky words and color the flowers using either brown, or pink.

does · made · their · once · upon · always

My Best Story

Moat Farm: read the words below and then use them to complete the story.

lives   Neb   Ben   Farm   sheep

Green   sheepdogs   hill   truck

1.

This is Moat _____ .

2.

Farmer Green

_____

on Moat Farm.

3.

Ben and Neb are

_____ .

4.

_____ and _____
help on the farm.

5.

This morning, Ben

and Neb run up

the _____ and

help round up...

6.

...the _____ .

7.

Farmer _____
checks that the sheep
are well.

8.

Neb and Ben rest
in the back of the

_____ .

38

helicopter   sister   numbers   cooker

girl   thirsty   third   bird

Saturday   purple   Thursday   hurt

Read the words and then write them in the correct /er/ spelling.

dinner

shirt

purse

letter

hurt

diver

first

turn

dinner

bird

fur

sister

girl

39

after

Write over the dotted letters and add the missing letters.

love   cover   after
l_v_   c_v__   _f_er
l___   __v_r   _____

Dictation:

_____

_____

_____

Finish these sentences by adding *love*, *cover*, or *after*.

I _____ to go swimming.

_____ that, we can have some chips.

The _____ of the book was torn.

Read the tricky words and color the flowers using a brown pen, or pencil.

once   upon   always   also   of   eight

40

Inky's Day
Out

Read the clues and write the answers in the crossword grid.

1. This will help you to find your way.
2. This heats food for you to eat.
3. A small insect that lives in a nest underground.
4. If you go camping, you may sleep in this.
5. You wash with _____ and water.
6. An animal that hisses.
7. The time of year when it is cold.
8. A chick hatches from this.
9. This is on the end of your arm.
10. A sort of stone.
11. The sky is blue and the trees are _____.
12. At night it is _____.

Write inside each lower-case letter and write the capital letter next to it.

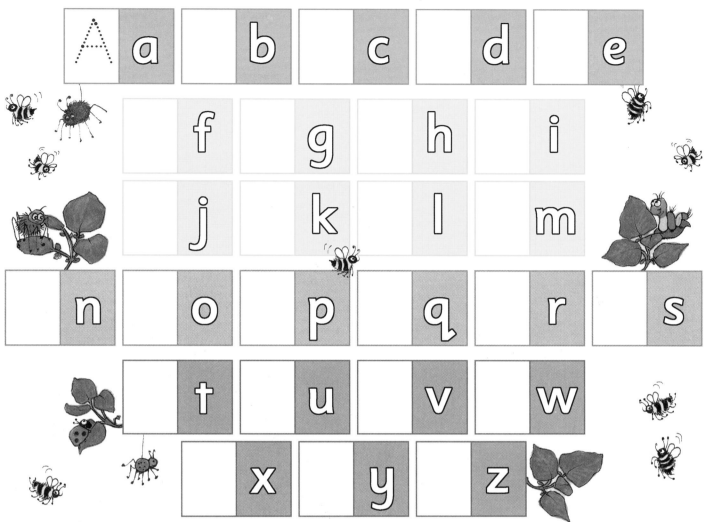

A a   b   c   d   e

f   g   h   i

j   k   l   m

n   o   p   q   r   s

t   u   v   w

x   y   z

Read each sentence and then color the picture to match.

The boy has a blue drum.   There are six red fish.

fairy   stairs   chair   pair

bear   wear   tear   pear

scarecrow   hare   square   dare

Read the words inside the salmon and join them to right bear. Color the pictures.

44

every   mother   Tricky words   father

Write over the dotted letters and add the missing letters.

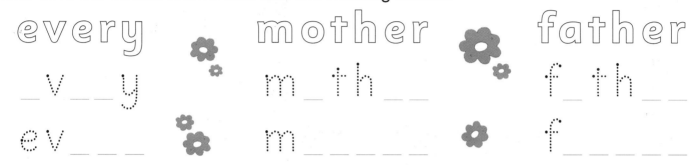

every   mother   father

_v___y   m_th__   f_th__

ev___   m_____   f_____

Finish these sentences by adding *every*, *mother*, or *father*.

My _____ and _____ are my parents.

I go dancing _____ week.

Dictation:

_____

_____

_____

Read the tricky words and color the flowers using a brown pen, or pencil.

also   of   eight   love   cover   after

In the old tree lived...

Read the story and answer the questions below.

Once upon a time, there was a king called Alfred. His wife was Queen Matilda. They lived in a castle, with a cat called Fluffy.

One night, King Alfred was hungry. So he got up and made himself some cheese sandwiches to eat. Some crumbs from the sandwich fell onto the floor.

A mouse saw the crumbs from her mouse hole in the corner of the room. She could have a midnight feast, if she was quick and quiet. She crept out, and had just reached the crumbs, when Fluffy looked into the room. The mouse ran for her hole as quickly as she could. Fluffy ran for the mouse as quickly as he could.

The mouse reached her hole hungry, but safe!

1. What is the king's name? _____

2. What is the queen's name? _____

3. What sort of animal is Fluffy? _____

4. What did King Alfred make to eat? _____

5. Who saw the crumbs on the floor? _____

6. Who saw the mouse? _____

7. Did the cat catch the mouse? _____

Complete the sentences writing about a recent birthday, or a holiday celebration. Illustrate what you write in the frames.

We had a party for _____

We ate some _____

_____

_____

_____

_____